ECCLESIASTES
Enjoying God's Gifts

I know that there is nothing better for men than to be happy and do good while they live. That everyone may eat and drink, and find satisfaction in all his toil—this is the gift of God. Ecclesiastes 3:12–13

By Kurt W. Brink

CPH
SAINT LOUIS

Edited by Julene Gernant Dumit

Series editors: Thomas J. Doyle and Rodney L. Rathmann

We solicit your comments and suggestions concerning this material. Please write to Product Manager, Adult Bible Studies, Concordia Publishing House, 3558 S. Jefferson Avenue, St. Louis, MO 63118-3968.

Scripture quotations are taken from the HOLY BIBLE, NEW INTERNATIONAL VERSION®. NIV®. Copyright © 1973, 1978, 1984 by International Bible Society. Used by permission of Zondervan Publishing House. All rights reserved.

Contents

Preface

My goal in preparing this study was to make available to all Christians the wealth of divine wisdom for daily living this book of the Bible contains.

The study guide is a topical, thematic, and categorized arrangement of Ecclesiastes. Because of the thematic arrangement, the same verses may appear under different categories.

The goals of this study are to discover the truths of Solomon, the wisest of men, and to guide students deeply into all of the Bible so that they may obtain all of the spiritual riches of our Savior from sin, Jesus Christ, who is the same yesterday, today, and forever.

I am grateful for the faithful assistance of a number of brother pastors in the Albuquerque area who critiqued the manuscript and made numerous suggestions for improving it. I am also deeply indebted to Mr. and Mrs. Bruce Wickesberg for typing the manuscript.

Lesson 1

The Author and Time

Theme Verse

"I have seen all the things that are done under the sun; all of them are meaningless, a chasing after the wind" (**Ecclesiastes 1:14**).

Goal

We seek to learn from Solomon how to view and live life in a sinful world, a world that sometimes seems meaningless.

What's Going On Here?

"He was wiser than any other man" (**1 Kings 4:31**)—thus the Scriptures describe the man the Holy Spirit used to give our world the precious biblical book of Ecclesiastes. King Solomon will supply readers with a wide variety of instruction in Christian truth and living. He addresses oft-repeated themes such as "under the sun," "meaningless, a chasing after the wind," and "time," which we will look at in this first lesson. Bon voyage!

Searching the Scriptures

The Author of Ecclesiastes

1. Read **Ecclesiastes 1:1, 12–13, 16.** What do these verses tell us about the author of Ecclesiastes? Compare **1 Kings 4:1, 29–34.** Although the book of Ecclesiastes never mentions Solomon by name, why is he a likely candidate for the authorship of this book?

2. Read **1 Kings 3:7–14.** Why did Solomon ask the Lord for wisdom? Read **1 Kings 3:16–26.** How did Solomon reveal his great wisdom as judge of Israel?

3. Despite his great wisdom, Solomon repeatedly did things that were very foolish and had grave consequences. Read **1 Kings 11:1–13.** What were the consequences of Solomon's foolish actions?

Read **Ecclesiastes 2:4–11.** Ecclesiastes seems to have been written late in the author's life. One of its main themes is the emptiness of life without God. Thus some scholars see in Ecclesiastes evidence that later in life Solomon repented of his idolatry.

Under the Sun

1. Solomon used the phrase "under the sun" 29 times. Read the following verses and describe what Solomon meant by that phrase: **Ecclesiastes 1:9; 2:17–19; 4:1–3; 6:12; 8:15; 9:3.**

2. Solomon's use of the term implies that there is something beyond life under the sun. Read **Revelation 21:1–3, 22–23.** What will be the role of the sun in that life?

Meaningless

Read **Ecclesiastes 1:2** and **12:8.** These two declarations frame the book of Ecclesiastes and proclaim one of its main themes. The Hebrew word rendered "meaningless" by the NIV is difficult to translate. Sometimes it is translated as "vanity." The literal meaning of the word carries the sense of something being transitory, of something having little lasting value. But as used in Ecclesiastes it seems also to mean something that is absurd, that makes no logical sense or goes against the way people normally think that life should work.

At times Solomon seems to have taken the perspective of someone who has no relationship with God. This perspective is especially prevalent in the first six chapters of the book. Some interpreters think Solomon did that in order to convince his hearers/readers of the futility of life apart from God. At other times Solomon seems to have been reflecting how absurd life in a fallen world can seem even to believers.

1. Read **1:14.** Solomon illustrated his point about meaningless life by using a word picture. How would you describe the action mentioned in this verse?

2. Read the following verses and note some of the specific things Solomon labeled as meaningless and why: **1:16–18; 2:17–21; 3:18–19; 5:10; 7:15; 8:14.** Based on these verses, what would you say is the root cause of this meaninglessness?

3. Read **3:12–13; 9:7–10; 12:13.** What is Solomon's advice for living in this fallen, often absurd world?

Time

1. Read **3:1–8.** What point is Solomon making here? How does this affect the way we approach life?

2. Read **3:11.** How does this sense of eternity set human beings apart from other creatures whom God gave life? What are all human beings aware of in light of this sense of eternity? Even so, under what limitations are human beings?

3. Read **7:14.** What does Solomon urge us to be when times are good? What are we to remember when times are bad? What may God's purpose be when He lets Christians experience bad times?

4. Read **7:17.** What are some reasons people die before their time is up? Read **9:11–12.** How does the reference to fish and birds remind us that daily they are only a breath away from meeting their Maker?

The Word for Us

1. How can Solomon's perspective on life in a sinful world and on time keep us from becoming disillusioned when life seems absurd?

2. Discuss the following: Christians should frequently utilize "a time to speak" (**3:7**) about their faith in Jesus.

3. In the case of Christians "a time to hate" (**3:8**) is *always* for which three-letter word? Why?

4. What situations in your life can you identify that occurred at the right time? Reflect on this statement: God's guiding hand has shaped my life.

Closing

Sing or read together the following stanzas of "All Depends on Our Possessing":

All depends on our possessing
God's free grace and constant blessing,
Though all earthly wealth depart.
They who trust with faith unshaken
By their God are not forsaken
And will keep a dauntless heart.

He who to this day has fed me
And to many joys has led me
Is and ever shall be mine.
He who did so gently school me,
He who daily guides and rules me
Will remain my help divine.

Well He knows what best to grant me;
All the longing hopes that haunt me,
Joy and sorrow, have their day.
I shall doubt His wisdom never;
As God wills, so be it ever;
I commit to Him my way.

If my days on earth He lengthen,
God my weary soul will strengthen;
All my trust in Him I place.
Earthly wealth is not abiding,
Like a stream away is gliding;
Safe I anchor in His grace.

Lesson 2

From Cradle to Grave

Theme Verse

"The dust returns to the ground it came from, and the spirit returns to God who gave it" **(Ecclesiastes 12:7).**

Goal

We seek to learn what Solomon teaches in Ecclesiastes about human life from birth to death.

What's Going On Here?

Here King Solomon writes about the common lot of all of us. We are born, we are young, and all too soon we are old. In due time death overtakes us and our loved ones, and our bodies are laid to rest on God's acre. We aren't remembered long by those who come after us, and they receive our estate; we can take nothing with us. Concerning Christians, however, the author says: "Man goes to his eternal home" **(12:5).**

Searching the Scriptures

Born

1. Read **1:4.** What is Solomon's point?

2. Read **3:1–2a.** State reasons why you are happy that God gave you the gift of physical life. How do Christians view their children? See **Psalm 127:3.** At what point will Christian parents begin the process of bringing up their children in the nurture and admonition of the Lord?

3. Read **Ecclesiastes 4:1–3.** On what basis did Solomon come to the conclusion that the person who hasn't been born yet is better off than both the living and the dead? See also **Jeremiah 20:14–18.** What further perspective is offered in **Romans 8:35–39?**

4. Read **Ecclesiastes 7:1.** Why is the day a Christian dies better than the day he or she was born? In the meantime, what can we confess with the apostle Paul **(Philippians 1:21–24)?**

Youth

Read **Ecclesiastes 11:9–12:1.** What things does Solomon urge young people to do in these verses? What does it mean to remember your Creator?

The Brevity of Life

1. Read **5:18–20.** Whom does Solomon credit for giving us human beings the gift of life, brief though it is? What other earthly blessings that we Christians enjoy are named as gifts from the Lord in **verse 19?** Why will believers not give much thought to their brief lives according to **verse 20?**

2. Reflect on the word picture Solomon uses to describe the shortness of life in **6:12?**

Aged

1. Read **11:8** and **12:1.** Why does the Lord, through Solomon, remind men and women who have lived many years that days of trouble are ahead of them?

Ecclesiastes 12:2–5 addresses the bodily infirmities, largely in picture language, that eventually, in greater or lesser degree, overtake all old people. Read these verses with the following interpretation in mind (taken from Roland Cap Ehlke, *Ecclesiastes/Song of Songs*, People's Bible Commentary, Concordia, 1992, pp. 120–22).

The first part of **verse 2** "points to the sadness of growing old. Friends and loved ones die. Loneliness and sickness set in. The days of productivity are past. Many an old person longs for the day he or she will leave the dark valley of life on earth.

" 'The clouds return after the rain [**v. 2b].**' When we are young sunshine follows the rain. But as life's sicknesses, heartaches and problems pile up, recovery doesn't come so quickly. An old person often gets through one sickness or trouble only to have another follow on its heels" (p. 120).

In **verse 3** the keepers represent the arms and hands, the strong men the legs. The grinders are the teeth. The last part of **verse 3** refers to the dimming of eyesight. **Verse 4** refers to the loss of hearing and the loss of sleep. The first part of **verse 5** pictures the fear many elderly face because they are vulnerable. Pale almond tree blossoms may suggest gray hair. The loss of desire might be for food or for sex. As a person goes to his or her eternal home, life on earth continues with professional mourners doing their job.

2. What do the words "Remember your Creator" urge Christian senior citizens to think about as their debilities increase?

Throughout Scripture our God speaks words of comfort, hope, and help to all believers, including the elderly. Referring to the following passages will be a blessing to the troubled and those who suffer when their Lord seems far away: **Psalm 71:5–9; 91:9–16; 94:18–19, 22; Isaiah 46:4; Matthew 28:20; Hebrews 13:5–6.**

Death—Unpredictable

Read **Ecclesiastes 7:14; 8:8; 9:12.** Even though the day of one's death is unpredictable, why can Christians live their lives each day with serene confidence? See **Psalm 31:5** and **John 14:1–3.**

Death

1. Read **Ecclesiastes 2:14–16.** Why do the wise have no grounds to be proud of their wisdom?

2. Read **3:19–21.** See the NIV text note for an alternate translation of **verse 21.** What curse brought death to people **(Genesis 3:19)?** Apart from what God has revealed in His Word, what can people know about their eternal destiny?

3. Read **Ecclesiastes 9:3–6.** What is Solomon's very uncomplimentary verdict on all human beings since the fall into sin? Once people are dead, what stake do they have in life under the sun, that is in life in this world? See also **1:11; 9:10.**

4. Compare **Ecclesiastes 5:13–15** to **Psalm 49:5–12, 16–20** and **Luke 12:13–21.** What advantage are riches to a dead person?

Look up these Bible references; they give comfort, assurance, and hope to believers in Jesus who are facing death: **John 3:16; John 11:25–26; John 14:1–6; 2 Corinthians 5:1–10.**

Life after Death
Read **Ecclesiastes 12:5–7.**
1. How do these verses loudly proclaim that there is indeed life after death?

2. To what do the picturesque phrases in **12:6** refer? What does Solomon again urge people to do before it is too late?

3. Read **Revelation 21:1–4.** Describe the eternal home of those who die in the Lord.

The Word for Us

1. How will Christian people handle the enjoyment of life Solomon speaks about in **8:15?** What does the last half of this verse say about the joy believers experience during their life?

2. The brevity of life should lead Christians to get beyond saying, "I'm going to ..." See **James 4:13–15.** In this connection, reflect on this saying: "Today is mine; tomorrow may not come!"

Closing

Sing or read together "In God, My Faithful God":

In God, my faithful God,
I trust when dark my road;
Great woes may overtake me,
Yet He will not forsake me.
It is His love that sends them;
At His best time He ends them.

My sins fill me with care,
Yet I will not despair.
I build on Christ, who loves me;
From this rock nothing moves me.
To Him I will surrender,
To Him, my soul's defender.

If death my portion be,
It brings great gain to me;
It speeds my life's endeavor
To live with Christ forever.
He gives me joy in sorrow,
Come death now or tomorrow.

"So be it," then, I say
With all my heart each day.
Dear Lord, we all adore You,
We sing for joy before You.
Guide us while here we wander
Until we praise You yonder.

Lesson 3

The Creator and Sinful Creatures

Theme Verses

"Now all has been heard; here is the conclusion of the matter: Fear God and keep His commandments, for this is the whole duty of man. For God will bring every deed into judgment, including every hidden thing, whether it is good or evil" **(Ecclesiastes 12:13–14).**

Goal

We seek to learn from Solomon about God, about how we are to respond to Him, about sin, and about His abundant grace and mercy demonstrated in the person and work of Jesus.

What's Going On Here?

Our life is a gift from God, says Solomon. He is our Lord, our Sustainer, and our Judge. The whole creation proclaims His majesty. He desires that we revere Him and keep His commandments. In this lesson we also look at what Solomon has to say about the sin that separates us from our Creator.

Searching the Scriptures

The Creator's Majesty

Read **Ecclesiastes 1:5–7.** How do these verses reflect the majesty of the Creator of all the things mentioned?

God

1. Read **3:11; 9:9; 11:5.** What do these verses tell us about God?

2. Read **3:14; 5:7; 7:16–18; 8:12–13; 12:13.** Solomon calls us to fear God (the Hebrew word used in all of these passages is the same). What does it mean to fear God? See also **Psalm 34:8–14; 103:8–14.**

3. What is Solomon's conclusion in **Ecclesiastes 12:13?** Who enables Christians to do this as a fruit of the Gospel **(Philippians 2:13)?**

4. Read **Ecclesiastes 9:1.** Who are the righteous? What comfort does this verse hold for Christians?

5. Read **2:24–25.** What is necessary to truly enjoy the blessings that come from God's hands?

6. Compare **Ecclesiastes 5:18–20** with **1 Timothy 6:6–10.** What precious gift does God grant to those who trust in Him to meet their every need?

7. Read **Ecclesiastes 6:12; 7:14; 8:7; 10:14.** While Christians do not know the future, what wonderful comfort do they have so far as the future is concerned? See **Psalm 31:15; Deuteronomy 33:27; John 14:18; Isaiah 54:10.**

8. Read **Ecclesiastes 3:17; 11:9; 12:14.** Which people will be judged according to **3:17?** How many people will be able to escape the Last Judgment? With whose righteousness will believers be clothed on Judgment Day? Who alone knows when the Last Day will come **(Matthew 24:36, 42)?**

Sin

1. Read **Ecclesiastes 7:20; 9:3.** How many human beings are afflicted with the spiritually deadly disease of sin according to **7:20?** What result of sin is mentioned in **9:3?** See also **Romans 6:23.**

2. How can we be saved from our sins and from their consequence—eternal death **(Romans 6:23; Acts 16:30–31)?**

Because we Christians are constantly attacked by the devil, the godless world, and our own sinful heart we need to pray these prayers frequently each day: **Psalm 50:15; 51:1, 10.**

The Word for Us

1. Why is it often a great blessing that Christians do not know the future? How does worrying about the future help or hinder us?

2. What do Christians know about those who claim to be able to foretell the future? Why is consulting such individuals "just for fun" evil? See **Leviticus 20:6; Deuteronomy 18:10–12.**

3. Read **Romans 14:9–12.** How should the knowledge that we will stand before the judgment seat of God affect our relationships with other people?

Closing

Sing or read together "We Praise You, O God":

We praise You, O God, our Redeemer, Creator;
In grateful devotion our tribute we bring.
We lay it before You, we kneel and adore You;
We bless Your holy name, glad praises we sing.

We worship You, God of our fathers, we bless You;
Through trial and tempest our guide You have been.
When perils o'ertake us, You will not forsake us,
And with Your help, O Lord, our struggles we win.

With voices united our praises we offer
And gladly our songs of thanksgiving we raise.
With You, Lord, beside us, Your strong arm will guide us.
To You, our great Redeemer, forever be praise!

Lesson 4

Christian, Enjoy Life

Theme Verses

"Moreover, when God gives any man wealth and possessions, and enables him to enjoy them, to accept his lot and be happy in his work—this is a gift of God. He seldom reflects on the days of his life, because God keeps him occupied with gladness of heart" **(Ecclesiastes 5:19–20).**

Goal

We seek to learn from Solomon how to enjoy our earthly lives and use the gifts God has given us to His glory.

What's Going On Here?

The author sums up the content of this lesson briefly and beautifully in the theme verses printed above. What do we Christians have that hasn't been given to us by our Lord? How should we view those gifts from the perspective of eternity and use them in ways that glorify God? These questions are the focus of our study in this lesson.

Searching the Scriptures

Christian, Enjoy Life

1. Read **Ecclesiastes 2:24–25; 3:12–13; 5:18–20.** What role does God play in our enjoyment of life? According to Solomon, what core things has God given us in which we can find enjoyment?

2. Reflect on Isaiah's warning in **Isaiah 5:11–16** to those who misuse God's good gifts.

3. Read **Ecclesiastes 2:26.** Those who please God are believers. See **Hebrews 11:6.** What gifts do these people receive from God's hand? What is the fate of sinners (in this context unbelievers)?

4. While God has given us food and drink to enjoy, why are we not to be worried about getting and keeping them? See **Matthew 6:25–34; Romans 14:17–18.**

Work

1. Read **Genesis 2:15.** Work was part of life in the Garden of Eden. But what happened to the nature of work after Adam and Eve sinned (**Genesis 3:17–19**)?

2. Solomon recognized that in this sinful world, work sometimes seems meaningless. Read **Ecclesiastes 2:18–23; 4:4; 5:15; 6:7.** What things made work seem meaningless to Solomon?

3. Nevertheless, we live in this fallen world and work is a substantial part of our lives. What did Solomon conclude about how we should approach our work **(3:22)?** Why? From whom do we receive the ability to do that **(2:24)?**

Accomplishments

1. Read **Ecclesiastes 2:4–11.** Solomon was a great man who accomplished many things, yet when he surveyed those accomplishments what did he conclude? Why?

2. Regardless of how we view our accomplishments, what comfort does Solomon offer in **9:1?**

3. What important reminder is given Christians in **Psalm 127:1?** How do the closing words of the Lord's Prayer give expression to this truth?

Wealth

1. Read **Ecclesiastes 5:19.** Who is the source of a person's wealth? According to **6:2** what else is necessary for a person to enjoy his or her wealth?

2. Read **5:10–17.** Explain the difference between being wealthy and loving money. Why are those who love money never satisfied? See also **1 John 2:15–17.**

3. Reflect on Solomon's penetrating question in **Ecclesiastes 5:11.** What robs some people of sleep **(5:12)?**

4. Read **Matthew 6:19–21, 24–34.** Describe the attitude toward money that the Lord enables His followers to have?

The Word for Us

1. One way to use God's gifts in a manner that pleases Him is to thank Him for them. Discuss ways we can keep our prayers before meals from becoming empty words (see **Matthew 15:8**).

2. What is to be said for doing our earthly calling with all our might, as Solomon encourages in **Ecclesiastes 9:10?** See also **Colossians 3:23–24.** Is there such a thing as carrying that advice too far?

Closing

Sing or read together "Forth in Your Name, O Lord, I Go":

Forth in Your name, O Lord, I go,
My daily labor to pursue,
You, only You, resolved to know
In all I think or speak or do.

The task Your wisdom has assigned,
Oh, let me cheerfully fulfill;
In all my works Your presence find
And prove Your good and perfect will.

You may I find at my right hand,
Whose eyes see truly what I do,
And labor on at Your command
And offer all my works to You.

Give me to bear Your easy yoke
And ev'ry moment watch and pray
And still to things eternal look
And hasten to Your glorious day.

For You I joyously employ
Whatever You in grace have giv'n;
I run my course with even joy,
I closely walk with You to heav'n.

Lesson 5

Worship and Wisdom

Theme Verse

"Guard your steps when you go to the house of God. Go near to listen rather than to offer the sacrifice of fools, who do not know that they do wrong" (Ecclesiastes 5:1).

Goal

We seek to learn what Solomon has to teach us about worship and wisdom.

What's Going On Here?

Lesson 5 addresses the all-important subject of Christian worship and sternly warns against heartless worship the author calls "the sacrifice of fools" (5:1). Also treated by King Solomon are wisdom and the differences between the wise and the foolish.

Searching the Scriptures

Pitfalls in Worship

Read Ecclesiastes 5:1–7.

1. How does Solomon urge us to approach worship in 5:1? What attitude does he warn against? See also 1 Samuel 15:22; Matthew 15:7–9.

2. Why is the psalmist's prayer recorded in **Psalm 19:14** important for all Christians to pray as they enter God's house of worship?

3. Vows were part of the worship life of God's Old Testament people. In most cases people were not required to make vows, but once vows were made, they were not to be broken (unless the vow involved doing something sinful and foolish). Discuss the vows people make today. How do Solomon's words in **5:4–7** speak to keeping those vows?

Wisdom

1. Read **Ecclesiastes 2:26; 12:11.** Who is the source of true wisdom? For that reason, what is its effect on people?

2. Read **7:11–12.** Discuss how wisdom can preserve people's lives. How does the wisdom recorded in the Scriptures preserve our lives for eternity? See **2 Timothy 3:15; John 20:31.**

3. Read **Ecclesiastes 9:11, 13–16; 10:1.** Why will true wisdom not necessarily be recognized by the world or rewarded in this life?

4. Read **8:16–17.** What limits are there on human wisdom?

Wisdom vs. Foolishness

1. Read **Ecclesiastes 2:12–16; 7:1–4.** What do the wise and the foolish have in common? How does Solomon contrast them?

2. Read **7:5–6; 9:17; 10:12–15.** Which—a wise person or a fool—makes a better advisor? Why? Who is our ultimate wisdom from God **(1 Corinthians 1:30)?**

The Word for Us

1. Compare **Ecclesiastes 5:2–3** with **Matthew 6:7–8.** Why are long prayers not necessarily pleasing to God?

2. Read **James 3:13–18.** Discuss how the characteristics mentioned by James show true wisdom. Who best exemplifies that wisdom and gives it to us?

Closing

Sing or read together the following stanza of "Oh, Come, Oh, Come, Emmanuel":

Oh, come, our Wisdom from on high,
Who ordered all things mightily;
To us the path of knowledge show,
And teach us in her ways to go.
Rejoice! Rejoice! Emmanuel
Shall come to you, O Israel!

Lesson 6

The Bad and the Good

Theme Verses

"Patience is better than pride. Do not be quickly provoked in your spirit, for anger resides in the lap of fools" (**Ecclesiastes 7:8–9**).

Goal

We seek to learn what Solomon has to teach us about dealing with the good and the bad in life.

What's Going On Here?

This lesson looks at the bad—vices like pride, oppression, and never being satisfied—and also at the good—virtues like patience, helping others, and generosity.

Searching the Scriptures

The Bad

1. Read **Ecclesiastes 10:16–18.** What is so bad about having government officials who are more interested in partying than governing? See also **Proverbs 31:4–5.** How will alcohol abuse affect the ability of anyone to carry out their God-given responsibilities? What are the dangers of laziness?

2. As Solomon says, we are blessed if our government officials are of noble character **(Ecclesiastes 10:17).** But even if they are not what do we owe them **(8:2–6; Romans 13:1–2)?** What is the exception to that duty **(Acts 5:29)?** What is the basis for Solomon's advice in **Ecclesiastes 10:20?**

3. Read **Ecclesiastes 7:9.** According to Solomon, why are we not to get angry quickly? What do we reflect when, by God's power working in us, we are slow to anger **(Jonah 4:2)?**

4. Read **Ecclesiastes 7:8.** What is the corrective for pride according to **Philippians 2:1–11?** Who enables us to do that **(Philippians 4:13)?**

5. What does Solomon warn against in **Ecclesiastes 7:7?** Why?

6. Read **Ecclesiastes 4:1; 5:8.** In what ways is **Psalm 56:1–13** sweet comfort for the oppressed who look to the Lord?

7. Read **Ecclesiastes 7:21–22.** What is Solomon's secret for having selective hearing? How might this secret help us?

The Good

1. Read **Ecclesiastes 7:1.** Reflect on why a good name is such a blessing.

2. Read **Ecclesiastes 4:9–12.** Reflect on the blessing God has given us in the help of others. How can pride keep us from giving or receiving help? Why do we need others to aid us in our Christian life **(Hebrews 10:24–25)?**

3. Read **Ecclesiastes 7:14.** What does Solomon encourage us to do when times are good? when they are bad? Life is a blend of good and evil days. Discuss how St. Paul handled this reality **(Philippians 4:10–13).**

4. Read **Ecclesiastes 7:8–9.** Who works the fruit of patience in the lives of Christians **(Galatians 5:22–23)?** How does patience help us in being slow to anger?

5. Read **Ecclesiastes 7:10.** How will following Solomon's advice in this verse help us to be "content in any and every situation" **(Philippians 4:12)?**

6. Compare **Ecclesiastes 11:1–2** with **Luke 6:38** and **14:13–14.** What characterizes the followers of Jesus? What does this aspect of their lives reflect and from whom does it flow **(John 1:16)?**

The Word for Us

1. Rather than curse those who rule **(Ecclesiastes 10:20),** what ought Christian citizens do **(1 Timothy 2:1–3)?**

2. What does God's Word say to able-bodied individuals who are idle and lazy by choice **(2 Thessalonians 3:10–12; 1 Timothy 5:13)?**

3. How does **Ecclesiastes 8:11** speak to our society?

4. Read **Ecclesiastes 4:8.** Does this description fit people in our world today? How does the Christian life differ **(1 Timothy 6:6–10, 17–19)?**

Closing

Sing or read together " 'Come, Follow Me,' Said Christ, the Lord":

"Come, follow Me," said Christ, the Lord,
"All in My way abiding;
Your selfishness throw overboard,
Obey My call and guiding.
Oh, bear your crosses, and confide
In My example as your guide.

"I am the light; I light the way,
A godly life displaying;
I help you walk as in the day;
I keep your feet from straying.
I am the way, and well I show
How you should journey here below.

"My heart is rich in lowliness;
My soul with love is glowing;
My lips the words of grace express,
Their tones all gently flowing.
My heart, my mind, my strength, my all
To God I yield; on Him I call.

"I teach you how to shun and flee
What harms your soul's salvation;
Your heart from ev'ry guile to free,
From sin and its temptation.
I am the refuge of the soul
And lead you to your heav'nly goal."

Then let us follow Christ, our Lord,
And take the cross appointed
And, firmly clinging to His word,
In suff'ring be undaunted.
For those who bear the battle's strain
The crown of heav'nly life obtain.

ECCLESIASTES
Enjoying God's Gifts

Leaders Notes

Preparing to Teach Ecclesiastes

In preparation to teach, consult introductions to the book of Ecclesiastes (such as the one in the *Concordia Self-Study Bible*), and if possible read the People's Bible Commentary volume on Ecclesiastes entitled *Ecclesiastes/Song of Songs*, available from Concordia Publishing House. Another excellent resource is *Exposition of Ecclesiastes* by H. C. Leupold, Baker Book House, 1952. Although it is not strictly a commentary, the section on Ecclesiastes in *The Word Becoming Flesh* by Horace Hummel (Concordia, 1979) also contains much that is of value for the proper interpretation of this biblical book. Hummel answers arguments made by Leupold and others against solomonic authorship.

Also read the text in a modern translation. The NIV is generally referred to in the lesson comments. The NIV shows clear paragraph divisions, the structure of the book, and the poetic form in which much of Ecclesiastes is written.

In the section "Searching the Scriptures," the leader serves as a guide, using the questions given (or others) to help the class discover what the text actually says. This is a major part of teaching, namely, directing the learners to discover for themselves. Another major portion of each lesson is helping the students by discussion to see the meaning for our times, for the church and world today, and especially for our own lives.

Group Bible Study

Group Bible study means mutual learning from one another under the guidance of a leader or facilitator. The Bible is an inexhaustible resource. No one person can discover all it has to offer. In a class many eyes see many things and can apply them to many life situations. The leader should resist the temptation to "give the answers" and so act as an "authority." This teaching approach stifles participation by individual members and can actually hamper learning. As a general rule the teacher is not to "give interpretation" but to "develop interpreters." Of course there are times when the leader should and must share insights and information gained by his or her own deeper research. The ideal class is one in which the leader guides class members through the lesson and engages them in meaningful sharing and discussion at all points, leading them to a summary of the lesson at the close. As a general rule, don't explain what the learners can discover by themselves.

The general aim of every Bible study is to help people grow spiritually, not merely in biblical and theological knowledge, but also in Christian thinking and living. This means growth in Christian attitudes, insights, and skills for Christian living. The focus of this course must be the church and the world of our day. The guiding question will be, What does the Lord teach us for life today through the book of Ecclesiastes?

Teaching the Old Testament

Teaching the Old Testament can degenerate into mere moralizing, in which do-goodism becomes a substitute for the Gospel and sanctification gets confused with justification. Actually the justified sinner is not moved by Law but by God's grace to a totally new life. His or her faith in Christ is always at work in every context of life. Meaningful personal Christianity consists of faith flowing from God's grace and is evidenced in love for other people. Having experienced God's free grace and forgiveness, the Christian daily works in his or her world to reflect the will of God for humanity in every area of human endeavor.

The Christian leader is Gospel oriented, not Law oriented. He or she distinguishes Law from Gospel. Both are needed. There is no clear Gospel unless we first have been crushed by the Law and see our sinfulness. There is no genuine Christianity where faith is not followed by life pleasing to God. In fact, genuine faith is inseparable from life. The Gospel alone creates in us the new heart that causes us to love God and our neighbor.

When Christians teach the Old Testament, they do not teach it as a "lawbook," but instead as books containing both Law and Gospel. They see the God of the Old Testament as a God of grace who out of love establishes a covenant of mercy with His people **(Deut. 7:6–9)** and forgives their sins. Christians interpret the Old Testament using the New Testament message of fulfilled prophecy through Jesus Christ. They teach as leaders who personally know the Lord Jesus as Savior, the victorious Christ who gives all believers a new life **(2 Cor. 5:17)** and a new mission **(John 20:21)**.

Pace Your Teaching

Do not try to cover every question in each lesson. This attempt would lead to undue haste and frustration. Be selective. Pace your teaching. Spend no more than five minutes with "Theme Verse" and "Goal" and two or three minutes with "What's Going On Here?" Allow 20 minutes to apply the lesson ("The Word for Us") and five minutes for "Closing." This schedule, you will notice, allows only about 30 minutes for working with the text ("Searching the Scriptures").

Should your group have more than a one-hour class period, you can take it more leisurely. But do not allow any lesson to "drag" and become tiresome. Keep it moving. Keep it alive. Keep it deeply meaningful. Eliminate some questions and restrict yourself to those questions most meaningful to the members of the class. If most members study the text at home, they can report their findings, and the time gained can be applied to relating the lesson to life.

Good Preparation

Good preparation by the leader usually affects the pleasure and satisfaction the class will experience.

Suggestions to the Leader for Using the Study Guide

The Lesson Pattern

The material in this guide is designed to aid *Bible study*, that is, a consideration of the written Word of God, with discussion and personal application growing out of the text at hand. The typical lesson is divided into these sections:

1. "Theme Verse"
2. "Goal"
3. "What's Going On Here?"
4. "Searching the Scriptures"
5. "The Word for Us"
6. "Closing"

"Theme Verse" and "Goal" give the leader assistance in arousing the interest of the group in the concepts of the chapter. Do not linger too long over the introductory remarks. Merely show that the material to be studied is meaningful to Christian faith and life today.

"What's Going On Here?" helps you gain an understanding of the textual portion to be considered in the session. Before the text is broken down for closer scrutiny, it should be seen in the perspective of a greater whole. At this point the class leader takes the participants to a higher elevation to show them the general layout of the lesson. The overview gives the group an idea where it is going, what individual places are to be visited, and how the two are interrelated.

"Searching the Scriptures" provides the real "spadework" necessary for Bible study. Here the class digs, uncovers, and discovers; it gets the facts and observes them. Comment from the leader is needed only to the extent that it helps the group understand the text. The questions in the study guide are intended to help the learners discover the meaning of the text.

Having determined what the text says, the class is ready to apply the message. Having heard, read, marked, and learned the Word of God, we proceed to digest it inwardly through discussion, evaluation, and application. This is done, as the study guide suggests, by taking the truths of Ecclesiastes and applying them to the world and Christianity in general and then to personal Christian life. Class time may not permit discussion of all questions and topics.

Remember, the Word of God is sacred, but the study guide is not. The guide offers only suggestions. The leader should not hesitate to alter the guidelines or substitute others to meet his or her needs and the needs of the participants. Adapt your teaching plan to your class and your class period. Good teaching directs the learner to discover for himself or herself. For the teacher this means directing the learner, not giving the learner answers. Choose the verses that should be looked up in Scripture. What discussion questions will you ask? At what points? Write them in the margin of your study guide. Involve class members, but give them clear directions.

Begin the class with prayer, and allow for a brief time of worship at the end of the class session. Suggestions for closing devotions are given in the study guide. Remember to pray frequently outside of class for yourself and your class. May God the Holy Spirit bless your study and your leading of others into the comforting truths of God's Christ-centered Word.

Lesson 1

The Author and Time

The Class Session

Have volunteers read the "Theme Verse," "Goal," and "What's Going On Here?"

Searching the Scriptures

The Author of Ecclesiastes

1. From Ecclesiastes we learn that the author was known as the Teacher, that he was a son of David, that he was king over Israel in Jerusalem, and that he had devoted himself to the study of wisdom. Solomon fits all these criteria. He was especially well known for the great wisdom that the Lord had given him.

2. Solomon asked for a discerning heart so that he could wisely govern the people God had entrusted to him. The wisdom God gave him was evident in his ability to distinguish who indeed was the child's mother in the incident recorded in **1 Kings 3:16–26.**

3. Solomon married many foreign women who led him away from total devotion to the Lord and into idolatry. As a consequence, the Lord would divide Solomon's kingdom and give most of it to one of his subordinates. Note that in His grace and for the sake of David and Jerusalem, the Lord would reserve one tribe for the descendants of Solomon.

Under the Sun

1. Solomon used the phrase "under the sun" to refer to this life—life on earth—with all of its limitations.

2. In heaven God will dwell with His people and give them light. Therefore there will be no need for the sun.

Meaningless

1. "Chasing after the wind" is a futile activity, a further description of meaningless life, especially if one does not have the perspective of eternity.

2. **1:16–18**—Wisdom itself, when one really understands how the world works, especially apart from God, leads to grief. Note that in other places in Ecclesiastes (such as **7:11–12**) and in Proverbs Solomon talked about the virtues of wisdom.

2:17–21—Death robs a person of the opportunity to enjoy the fruits of his or her labors, which are then left to someone who did not earn them.

3:18–19—People as well as animals die, and thus without God and the hope of everlasting life, the span of their life is meaningless.

5:10—Wealth is meaningless because those who have it are never satisfied.

7:15; 8:14—The injustice of a wicked person being treated as a righteous person is absurd, meaningless.

The root cause of all this meaninglessness is sin, sin which causes injustice and reaps death.

3. Solomon's advice is to be happy, to do good, to enjoy the earthly blessings God has given—food, wine, clothing, family, work—and to fear God and keep His commandments.

Time

1. Some of the activities in Solomon's list are behaviors over which people have some control. Others are totally beyond their control—such as the time of their birth. Thus Solomon's point seems to be that all events are in the hands of God. When we view life from that perspective we can accept the bad times as well as the good, knowing that nothing that happens to us is beyond God's knowledge and control and that God will be with us and strengthen us in all things.

2. God set human beings apart from other living creatures by giving them a sense that there is something beyond this life. This includes a knowledge about God that can be deduced from the created world. In the words of Paul, "What may be known about God is plain to them, because God has made it plain to them. For since the creation of the world God's invisible qualities—His eternal power and divine nature—have been clearly seen, being understood from what has been made, so that men are without excuse" **(Rom. 1:19–20).** This is called general knowledge of God. Yet even with that knowledge human beings cannot understand what God has done from the beginning to the end. They especially know nothing of the salvation God has worked for them in Christ apart from the Scriptures, where God has revealed that special knowledge.

3. Solomon urges us to be happy when times are good and, as was discussed in question 1 above, to remember when times are bad that all of our times are in the hands of our gracious God. Answers will vary. God sometimes allows bad to happen to His children to teach them and to help them become the people He has recreated them to be in Christ.

4. People sometimes die before their time is up because they are foolish or wicked. Like fish and birds that are easily ensnared, we too may be overtaken by evil times and stand before God at a time when we least expected to die.

The Word for Us

1. Sin, Satan, and evil have totally corrupted this world, and thus, at times, life seems absurd. Although we see life from the perspective of those who know and love God, we would be naive to think that the absurdity of life will never affect us. But even when life seems meaningless we can enjoy God's gifts and say with the psalmist: "But I trust in You, O LORD; I say, 'You are my God.' My times are in Your hands" **(Psalm 31:14–15).**

2. Answers will vary. As Peter tells us, we are always to be prepared to share the Gospel **(1 Peter 3:15).**

3. Christians are always to hate sin.

4. Answers will vary.

Closing

Follow the suggestion in the study guide.

Lesson 2
From Cradle to Grave

The Class Session

Have volunteers read the "Theme Verse," "Goal," and "What's Going On Here?"

Searching the Scriptures

Born

1. In contrast to the seeming permanence of the earth, human life is very short. One generation quickly follows another.

2. Answers will vary. Christians view their children as gifts from the Lord and will want to begin immediately after the children are born to teach them to know and love the Lord. Many parents begin this process as they bring their infant children to the baptismal font, where through water and God's Word a child receives the gift of saving faith in Jesus and its blessings—forgiveness of sin and eternal life.

3. Because of the oppression taking place in this sinful world, Solomon reached the conclusion that the person who had not yet been born was the best off. Jeremiah, after suffering much, wished that he had never been born. While suffering may threaten to overwhelm us, and we may indeed wish we had never been born, we can put our faith in the promise of God recorded in **Romans 8:35–39**—nothing including injustice and suffering can separate us from His love in Christ Jesus, who suffered injustice, humiliation, and death for our sakes.

4. On the day we die, we go to be with the Lord, but with Paul we can confess that the Lord has things for us to do on earth until the day He takes us home.

Youth

Solomon urges young people to find and cultivate true joy. He enjoins them to follow their hearts' desires, but he tempers that by reminding them that God will judge them for all their actions. Finally he tells them where true and lasting joy can be found—in their Creator—and he urges them to remember Him while they are young, lest days of trouble cause them to turn their backs on God.

God is not satisfied that we simply remember him as we might some fact of history or bit of trivia. To remember him means to keep him and his word constantly in mind and heart, to trust in him and live each new day with him and for him. It means to be thankful for all his gifts and promises and to call on him in time of need (Roland Cap Ehlke, *Ecclesiastes/Song of Songs*, People's Bible Commentary, Concordia, 1992, pp. 119–20).

The Brevity of Life

1. Life comes from the hand of God. We also receive from His hand wealth and possessions, the ability to enjoy them, acceptance of our lot in life, and happiness in our work. We will not dwell on the brevity of our life because God occupies us with gladness of heart.

2. Solomon describes our life as passing like a shadow. Answers will vary. Elderly folks sometimes speak of the brevity of life thus: "The years pass by so quickly; it seems like only yesterday that I was a little child, playing with my brothers and sisters."

Aged

1. Our Lord wants His people to be prepared for the problems they will face as their bodies grow older and feebler and as their enjoyment of life begins to dim. Our Lord does not want His people of any age to have the unrealistic expectation that they will be untouched by the hardship and grief caused by sin and death.

2. Our Lord has promised to be with us and help us throughout all of our life. As we focus on Him and the promises He gives in His Word, He gives us much strength, encouragement, and hope. Reread Ehlke's definition of what it means to remember your Creator, quoted in "Youth" above.

Death—Unpredictable

As Christians we have committed our spirits into the loving hands of God. Our Lord Jesus has opened to us the way to everlasting life and gone to prepare a place for us with Him in heaven. Therefore we need not fear the day of our death (even if it should be today) but instead look forward to being with our Lord.

Death

1. Regardless of the advantages wisdom has, both the wise and the foolish die.

2. The curse of sin brought death into the world. Apart from the Word of God people can know nothing certain about their eternal destiny.

3. The sinful human heart is full of evil and madness. Once people are dead, they have no stake in this life and soon even the memory of them is forgotten. But Christians do well to have as their life's goal to serve Jesus and others in all ways they can, even though the world will not remember.

4. Riches provide no advantage at the time of death or thereafter.

Life after Death

1. **12:5** describes death as a person going to his or her eternal home, and **12:7** proclaims that when the body returns to the ground from which it came, the spirit returns to God who gave it.

2. The picture language in **12:6** refers to death. The silver cord and golden bowl refer to the preciousness of life and the pitcher and wheel to the usefulness of life. Solomon urges people to remember God, that is, cling to Him in faith, before they die and loose the opportunity.

3. In the new heaven and new earth, the eternal home of those who trust in the Lord Jesus for their salvation, God will dwell with His people and will wipe every tear from their eyes. In that home there will be no more death or mourning or crying or pain—none of the suffering brought to this earth by human sin.

The Word for Us

1. Christians enjoy the gifts of this life grateful to the God who has given them and mindful of the proper place of such gifts. By the grace of God we do not make idols of His gifts but use them in ways that are in accordance with His will. As we use God's gifts to His glory, joy accompanies our work in this life.

2. We should not be too confident or worried about tomorrow but rejoice in the day the Lord has given us today because it may indeed be our last on this earth.

Closing

Follow the suggestion in the study guide.

Lesson 3

The Creator and Sinful Creatures

The Class Session

Have volunteers read the "Theme Verses," "Goal," and "What's Going On Here?"

Searching the Scriptures

The Creator's Majesty

These verses witness to the complex and wondrous way in which God fashioned creation to run and thus proclaim His majesty.

God

1. God is the Creator of all things, whose ways are beyond our knowledge (**11:5**) or ability to fathom (**3:11**). God "has made everything beautiful in its time" (**3:11**). God has given all people life (**9:9**) and has placed in their hearts a sense of things eternal (**3:11**).

2. To fear God is to revere Him as Lord of the universe. Those whom God has made His children are not afraid of Him but hold Him in awe as their compassionate, gracious Father and order their lives according to His will.

3. Solomon concludes that people have no other purpose than to fear God and keep His commandments, something God's children are empowered to do by His Spirit.

4. As we will see later in the lesson, no one is righteous by nature. But for Jesus' sake, God has forgiven the sins of those who trust in Jesus and given them His righteousness. This verse proclaims the comforting truth that no matter what our future holds, our lives are in the hands of God.

5. Only in God, in knowing and loving Him, can people truly enjoy the life He has given with all of its blessings.

6. God grants His children the wonderful gift of contentment.

7. God, who does know the future, will be with us and support us with His unfailing love no matter what the future holds for us.

8. The righteous (believers) as well as the wicked (unbelievers) will stand before the judgment seat of God. Believers will be clothed in the righteousness of Christ. Only God the Father knows when the Last Day will be.

Sin

1. All people are sinful from the time of conception (**Ps. 51:5**).

Solomon mentions death, the result of sin, which afflicts all people.

2. We are saved by the grace of God through faith in Jesus, His Son, through whom He gives us the free gift of forgiveness and eternal life.

The Word for Us

1. Answers may vary. Knowing the future would likely scare us. Worrying, which shows a lack of trust in the Lord, hinders us spiritually and often physically, emotionally, and socially.

2. Those who claim to be able to foretell the future seek to go beyond the bounds God has set for people. Often those who make such claims are aided in their search by demonic forces. Consulting them, even "just for fun," amounts to allying oneself with the forces of evil.

3. Paul exhorts us, in view of the fact that we will all be judged by God, not to judge one another.

Closing

Follow the suggestion in the study guide.

Lesson 4
Christian, Enjoy Life

The Class Session
Have volunteers read the "Theme Verses," "Goal," and "What's Going On here?"

Searching the Scriptures
Christian, Enjoy Life
1. God gives us gifts to enjoy and the ability to enjoy them. Moreover, without Him, these gifts provide no real enjoyment **(2:25)**. According to Solomon, the core things God has given us to enjoy are food, drink, and satisfaction in our work.

2. Isaiah warns about the destruction that awaits those who abuse God's gifts and have no knowledge of the Giver.

3. God gives believers wisdom, knowledge, and happiness. Unbelievers on the other hand gather wealth only to eventually hand it over to those who have God's favor (believers).

4. The Lord has promised to meet our needs and wants us to seek what is much more important—His kingdom and righteousness—and to enjoy the benefits of being in that kingdom—Christ's righteousness, which has given us peace and joy in the Holy Spirit.

Work
1. Since the fall into sin, people need to work to meet their needs, and the work is difficult and beset with problems.

2. Industrious, wise people toil for a lifetime but must leave the fruit of their labors to someone else, and who knows how those people will use it **(2:18–22)**. Pain, grief, and a restless mind make work seem meaningless **(2:23)**. The envy that drives much human endeavor makes that endeavor seem meaningless **(4:4)**. A person can take nothing from his or her labors at death **(5:15)**. People work to satisfy their longings, but they always seem to want more and thus are never satisfied **(6:7)**.

3. Solomon concludes that we should find enjoyment in our work, since that is our lot. God enables us to find satisfaction in our work.

Accomplishments
1. Solomon concluded that all his accomplishments were meaningless and gained nothing.

2. Whether our accomplishments seem great or insignificant in our eyes

or in the eyes of the world, we can take comfort in knowing that they are in God's hands, and He will use them for His purposes.

3. **Psalm 127:1** reminds us that we are dependent on the Lord for the success of all of our accomplishments. He is the King of all; His is the power that enables our success; to Him be all the glory for all our accomplishments.

Wealth

1. The Lord is the source of everyone's wealth. In order for a person to enjoy wealth, that person must also be given the ability to enjoy it by God.

2. A person can be wealthy without being overly attached to money, while both rich and poor people can love money to the point of being obsessed by it. Riches can provide no lasting satisfaction, therefore those who seek such satisfaction from them will always be searching.

3. Answers will vary. Worrying about wealth can keep a person awake at night. Ask participants to share things that have kept them awake at night.

4. The Lord enables His followers to serve Him, being concerned about His kingdom and His righteousness and not worrying about having money or the things money can buy, knowing that the Lord will provide for their needs. The Lord enables His followers to care about storing up treasures in heaven that cannot be destroyed or taken away like earthly wealth can. Ask participants to share how these verses speak to anything that might cause us worry. Remind participants that God who loved them enough to send His only Son to die for their sins will love them enough to care for them at all times and in all circumstances.

The Word for Us

1. Answers will vary as participants consider ways to help themselves think about and mean what they say when they pray before meals.

2. Answers will vary. God has placed us in homes, jobs, communities, and congregations and has given us roles to fill in those vocations. When we give our vocations our best efforts, we serve Him. However, we need to keep all of our roles balanced, lest overzealousness in one area cause another area to lack. For instance, if we have any choice, we ought not work so hard and long (in our jobs or in our congregations) that our health or families suffer. Remind particpants that the Holy Spirit working through God's Word strengthens our faith, enabling us to keep balance in our life.

Closing

Follow the suggestion in the study guide.

Lesson 5

Worship and Wisdom

The Class Session

Have volunteers read the "Theme Verse," "Goal," and "What's Going On Here?"

Searching the Scriptures

Pitfalls in Worship

1. Solomon urges us to think about what we say and do as we worship ("guard your steps") and to listen. Remember that in worship God speaks to us through His Word. We should approach worship desiring to hear, believe, and obey that Word. Solomon warns against the sacrifice of fools, that is, hypocritical worship that just goes through the motions and is not accompanied by hearing, believing, and obeying the Word of God.

2. Out of our own resources we cannot offer God worship that is pleasing to Him. Instead, we rely on Him to guide our words and meditations in ways that please Him.

3. Some people tend to bargain with God when they are in difficult or dangerous situations. "If You rescue me, I will ..." Such vows are most likely attempts at manipulation. However, they should not be disregarded once a person has been rescued (unless they involve doing something sinful, in which case people should repent for having made them). God's people should not rashly make vows to God but should take the vows they do make with the utmost seriousness. One example of a serious vow that most of us have made is the vow we made at our confirmation to be faithful to God throughout our lives. Such vows, seriously taken and sincerely kept, are pleasing to God. The Holy Spirit working through God's Word strengthens our faith, enabling us to keep the vow made to him—to remain faithful until death.

Wisdom

1. God is the source of true wisdom. Like a shepherd, the Lord goads people with the wisdom He has recorded in Scripture.

> The words we have received from Solomon are more than mere human opinions. They are inspired by the Lord. Solomon likens them to "goads" and "embedded nails." Goads were sharp sticks for driving oxen or used by shepherds to prod their sheep forward. Like goads, the inspired Scriptures drive people to action. God's Word pricks our con-

---

science, pierces us to the heart, drives us to repentance and directs us to faith. While goads depict action, embedded nails symbolize stability. They hold things together and strengthen them. God's Word holds our lives together; it is our strength and stability. Indeed, it is the only solid foundation in this world of instability and change (Roland Cap Ehlke, *Ecclesiastes/Song of Songs*, People's Bible Commentary, Concordia, 1992, pp. 127–28).

2. Answers will vary. The Holy Spirit uses the message of the Gospel recorded in the Scriptures to create faith in Christ in human hearts and give those strength who have thus been made wise for salvation eternal life.

3. The folly and injustice that characterize this sinful world often seem to overwhelm wisdom and deny its possessors recognition and reward. For all wisdom's advantages in this life, those who possess it should not expect that their wisdom will always be recognized or rewarded here on earth. In fact true wisdom may bring persecution instead.

4. Human wisdom (at least in this life) will never be able to understand all the workings of the world.

Wisdom vs. Foolishness

1. The wise and the foolish share the common fate of all people—physical death **(Eccl. 2:16).** But the wise walk in the light while the foolish walk in the darkness **(2:13–14). 7:1–6**—The wise face the reality of death (and thus see their need for God). The wise know the value of suffering for building character (see **Rom. 5:1–5**). The foolish, on the other hand, laugh and party through life, denying the reality of death (and the judgment that follows).

2. The fool may sing a pleasant and attractive song **(7:5–6),** but the fool's advice at best is foolish and at worse is wicked madness **(10:13).** In contrast the words of the wise are gracious **(10:12),** and such a person will tell you what is in your best interest, even if that is a rebuke **(7:5).** The advice of the wise may be given in humble quietness, but it is worthy of being heeded in contrast to the loud words of a fool, even though the fool may be powerful **(9:17).** Our Lord Jesus Christ is the wisdom of God for us.

The Word for Us

1. God isn't pleased with lengthy, hasty prayers that are said to impress Him and to manipulate Him into granting requests. What pleases Him is when we approach Him in trust and reverence, knowing that He knows our needs before we tell Him and that He will take the best possible care of us.

2. Answers will vary. Students might try contrasting the characteristics with their opposites. **James 3:13**—True wisdom is not characterized by pride. **3:17**—Wisdom from God is not evil. It promotes harmony, not dissention. It is not rude or domineering. It is not unmerciful. It does not produce bad fruit. It does not play favorites. It is not phony or shallow. Jesus best exemplifies that wisdom and works that wisdom in us through the Holy Spirit who lives in our hearts **(2 Cor. 1:22)**.

Closing

Follow the suggestion in the study guide.

Lesson 6
The Bad and the Good

The Class Session

Have volunteers read the "Theme Verses," "Goal," and "What's Going On Here?"

Searching the Scriptures

The Bad

1. God has given government officials the great task of administering justice, something they will neglect if their primary concern is entertaining themselves with alcohol. The abuse of alcohol renders anyone unable properly to carry out their God-given roles in home, job, society, and congregation. Those who are lazy neglect the tasks that need to be done if life is to run relatively smoothly. They end up making life more difficult for themselves and others.

2. Because God has instituted human government, we owe that government obedience unless doing so would involve disobeying another command of God. We do so, knowing as Solomon says that there is a time for everything (**Ecclesiastes 8:5–6**) and thus even oppressive governments will come to an end and true justice will be rendered, if not in this life then in the life to come. Solomon advises us not even to curse those in authority over us in our thoughts or in the privacy of our bedrooms, lest what we said somehow reaches those we cursed.

3. We are not to become angry quickly because anger is characteristic of fools. This is not to say there is no time or place for anger, for there is. However, as sinful humans we most often get angry because things didn't go our way, not because an injustice has been done. When we are slow to anger we reflect the character of our gracious, compassionate God who is slow to anger.

4. Humbly serving others and considering their interests as Jesus did is the corrective for pride. Jesus Himself enables us to follow His lead in service. Remember, Jesus gave up everything to serve us, including His life, so that by His death on the cross we might have life eternal.

5. Solomon warns against extortion and bribes, which turn the wise into fools and corrupt the heart.

6. When David wrote this psalm he was miserably oppressed, yet he knew that with the Lord on his side whatever people did to him was of no eternal consequence.

7. When people say negative things about us we are likely to be hurt and offended. Remembering that many times we have said negative things about others will help us overlook small slights. And such remembering is one step in forgiving big offenses.

The Good

1. Answers will vary. A good reputation witnesses to the work God is doing in our lives through faith in Christ Jesus.

2. From the beginning God created people for companionship **(Gen. 2:18)**. If we think we can make it through this life without the support, encouragement, and assistance of others, we are pridefully and foolishly mistaken. As Solomon points out, we have limited resources, and there are many things in life we cannot do alone. We need others, not only to meet our physical, emotional, and social needs, but especially to encourage us in the faith and to spur us to the love and good deeds to which God has called us.

3. Solomon encourages us to be happy when times are good and to know that the Lord is in control and working out His purposes when they are bad. The Lord had taught St. Paul the secret of being content in all situations. God's grace revealed in Christ Jesus was sufficient to enable Paul to confess contentment in all situations.

4. The Holy Spirit works patience in the lives of believers. We are often quick to anger because we are impatient. Patience therefore aids us in being slow to anger.

5. Dwelling on the past and how much better it supposedly was only stirs up discontent in the present. So if we want to learn Paul's secret of being content, we will not dwell on the past; instead we will recall God's grace that we have in the present and into the future.

6. The followers of Jesus are characterized by generosity, especially toward the less fortunate. That generosity reflects the great generosity of Jesus, who willingly gave up His life on the cross for all sinners, from whom they receive the blessings they pass on to others. The generosity of believers will come back to them, but exactly how or when that will happen is up to God.

The Word for Us

1. Paul urges Christians to pray for those in authority over them. Note that Paul includes thanksgiving as well as intercession.

2. The Lord through Paul commands that those who are idle by choice should work and thus avoid the dangers of becoming gossips and busybodies.

3. Answers will vary. People in the United States see the truth of this verse as the justice system drags and crime becomes more prevalent.

4. Many people today are consumed with becoming and staying wealthy but find that they are never satisfied. The Christian in contrast is characterized by contentment with what the Lord has given, knowing that worldly wealthy has no lasting value and that seeking it can endanger one's soul. The only thing that we possess that has lasting consequence is our faith in Christ Jesus, which we have received solely by God's grace.

Closing

Follow the suggestion in the study guide.